Summary

of

David Brooks'

The Road to Character

By Eureka Books

The Road to Character | A Review

Table of Contents

OVERVIEW	3
IMPORTANT PEOPLE	5
ANALYSIS	7
Key Takeaway 1	7
Key Takeaway 2	10
Key Takeaway 3	12
Key Takeaway 4	14
Key Takeaway 5	16
Key Takeaway 6	18
Key Takeaway 7	20
Key Takeaway 8	23
Key Takeaway 9	25
Key Takeaway 10	27
Style Analysis	29
Perspective	31

OVERVIEW

David Brooks' *The Road to Character* examines how cultural and personal morals have altered over the last century, creating a world where virtues that were once considered poor character are now revered. However, despite this change in values, it is still possible to build a character that can rise above a focus on material possessions or personal successes.

Brooks presents a series of relatively brief, but detailed, biographies of several different people he believes demonstrate how leading a life of character is possible. The narrative arc of each story stretches from childhood to death, and in those stories are tales of the lows and struggles each individual experienced throughout their life. At some crucial moment, however, is a pivotal thought process or event that starts that individual on a road to character. The biographies show these people emulate character physically, mentally, and emotionally in their thoughts, actions, and dedication toward others, God, humanity, or some other ideal.

Characters, like Dorothy Day and Augustine, dedicated their lives to serving God, though both reached that end by living very different lives and served God in very different ways. George Eliot and Samuel Johnson were both writers dedicated to their craft and serving humanity in that context. Eliot often wrote of love. Johnson wrote of his faults, how working through them might help others recognize their own shortcomings and learn how to progress beyond them. Frances Perkins, A. Philip Randolph, and Bayard Rustin all dedicated themselves to political and social causes, labor and civil rights respectively, though each struggled in their own way in seeing their vision to the end.

These are just a few of the nine characters Brooks explores throughout the book, all of whom exemplify what a person of character and their road to developing character might look like. Brooks ties everything together with an examination of the progression of culture and the definition of character as well as a list of all of the components of good character that has lasted through the ages.

The Road to Character | A Review

IMPORTANT PEOPLE

David Brooks: Brooks is the author of the book, a pundit and columnist who was inspired to write the book to gain a clearer understanding of how to develop character and live a better life.

Frances Perkins: Perkins was a social activist in the early to mid-20th century who, at one point, served as secretary of labor under President Franklin Delano Roosevelt.

Dwight D. Eisenhower: Eisenhower was a US president who learned to restrain his fiery, passionate personality as he worked his way up through the military ranks and into the presidency.

Dorothy Day: Day was a devout Catholic organizer, social worker, and activist for the poor who created and managed *The Catholic Worker*, a Catholic newspaper and movement.

George Marshall: Marshall became army chief of staff during World War II, then secretary of state, and he held other government positions while training, inspiring, and organizing men to be victorious.

A. Phillip Randolph: Randolph was a civil rights activist who helped organize the August 28, 1963

March on Washington and other nonviolent protests. He served as a mentor to Bayard Rustin.

George Eliot: Born Mary Ann Evans, Eliot was a heralded novelist who chose true love shared with her husband, George Henry Lewes, over her social ties.

Augustine: Augustine was a fourth century writer and bishop who struggled to conform to Christianity. However, with the help of his devout mother, he embraced the faith wholeheartedly for the rest of his life.

Samuel Johnson: Johnson was a writer who suffered from physical and mental challenges in his childhood and early adulthood, but eventually became revered as a wise, accomplished individual.

ANALYSIS

Key Takeaways & Analysis of Key Takeaways

Key Takeaway 1

The definition of what character is and looks like has changed over time.

Analysis

Traditionally, character refers to traits like selflessness, humility, generosity, and self-sacrifice. While this definition persists in the minds of many, that definition has shifted somewhat to reflect the changing ideals of today. Nowadays, character might be used to describe traits like resilience, self-control, tenacity, and grit. These latter traits appear to be more focused on a person's ability to overcome obstacles and achieve success himself, while the former centers more on a person's ability to serve others.

The Road to Character | A Review

Today's society awards achievement in the working world. In this way, character could be seen as someone who succeeds at business but does not rub their successes in others' faces. While modesty is a traditional virtue of character building, the context is far different from the definition of character once seen in the past.

Other major cultural shifts have influenced the definition of character over the centuries. One such shift is information technology, particularly social media, that has exasperated a culture of self-celebration in the past decade. As many people take to social media as a way to promote themselves and share their opinions, character could be defined more along the lines of outward appearances, specifically those a person chooses to share about himself on social media.

The author describes today's society as lacking a moral vocabulary. As morals change, the way in which people describe morals can be lost in translation. In current society's moral vocabulary, people and institutions may be able to describe how to achieve success or build character, but often cannot describe why someone should do these things or why building character is important. They may understand external professional values but are unable to describe the difference between right and wrong or the internal values that govern goodness and how character is built.

Instead of self-contentedness, people continually seek outside approval to determine if what they are doing is moral rather than being able to determine their own morality based on their thoughts and actions and how they contribute to the betterment of society. Without a strong and vivid moral vocabulary, any definition of character, traditional or modern, can be lost in the fray.

Key Takeaway 2

The moral ecology of the day reflects the needs and views of society at that time and changes as society evolves.

Analysis

To define moral ecology often means looking at the needs and requirements of society at that time. A society creates a moral ecology surrounding a set of norms, assumptions, beliefs, habits, and behaviors that are encouraged and even institutionalized at that time. These moral codes of living are generally based on a collective response to the issues that society faces and the resources it has to address them, such as family, community, knowledge, art, and religion. What was considered fulfillment at a particular time was based on what society deemed to be a person's duty, and what that duty entailed was often decided on by an authority of some sort, such as a government or religious entity. Being a model citizen within the social status system at the time could mean being a product of the moral ecology at that time. As time goes on, the picture of a product of moral ecology can change.

In the culture of today's self-centered era, one of society's primary needs is success and the money, power, and prestige that comes along with it. In a hypercompetitive society, moral ecology centers around skills-building, self-advertising, or whatever can help someone get ahead in the world. That is not to say that today's society is entirely self-absorbed. Many people fight for good causes, such as the discrimination of minorities; lesbian, gay, bisexual, and transgender (LGBT) rights; equal pay for women; and rising up against major corporations and financial institutions.

However, an underlying sense of self does persist in so much of today's media, products, and even literature, particularly the rise of the self-help industry, all of which direct people to make themselves better than their current selves, their competition, or both. The moral ecology constructed by society will continue to evolve as society itself changes with each passing generation.

Key Takeaway 3

The culture of today is more concerned with mastering success rather than building character.

Analysis

Modern-day culture tends to focus more on development of career as well as the pursuit of money and success rather than the development of self and pursuit of character. Modern society focuses on resume virtues, the skills and abilities a person might bring to the job market, such as being tech-savvy, a winning salesman, or the ability to choose hot stocks. This is known as the concept of Adam 1.

In the past, this was not always so, as people tended to focus more on eulogy virtues, the lasting character impressions someone might refer to while describing someone at his funeral. Eulogy virtues include kindness, humility, and generosity. These virtues are described within the concept of Adam 2.

The author argues that there needs to be a balance between the traits of Adam 1 and the traits of Adam 2, though that is not the case in today's society. Competitive pressure has led to the importance of Adam 1, taking up most of people's energy, leaving little time, energy, and attention left to attend to developing Adam 2 virtues.

Part of this imbalance is the formation of today's meritocracy, wherein merit, or the ability to excel in the working world, is valued above all else, including eulogy virtues necessary to build character. This hypercompetitive culture has had subtle effects on values, character, and culture over the years as eulogy virtues are deemed less and less important. Cultivation of skills is ranked higher than cultivation of personality. The meritocracy encourages people to think about themselves, be sure of themselves, and sell themselves as the best of the group, causing character to fall to the wayside.

Key Takeaway 4

The road to character generally involves some sort of struggle in life that builds character through its progression and to its resolution.

Analysis

Character is not something a person is born with. It is not innate, and it is not automatic. Building character is a process and, generally, that process begins with, or at some point involves, a struggle. This struggle could be external, such as poverty, discrimination, and humiliation, or it could be internal, such as poor self-esteem, self-doubt, and other inner demons, such as greed or lust. Each individual's story chronicled in this book has a narrative arc that involves the person rising from the depths of an internal and/or external struggle and finding the entity within that they built true character upon.

While people may attain glory and exaltation with external achievements, such as winning wars, inventing technologies, or leading a civil rights movement, it is the internal struggle and achievements that truly build a person's character. After struggling with their own internal demons, people can show their true character, as those demons will present challenges that no army beyond the individual himself can surmount. Sin is inevitable and indivisible from human nature, so a person battling his own sins is commonplace. To win that battle in a way that the person grows and matures from it, and can then lead by example afterward, is to have developed lasting character.

Part of the internal struggle is the journey that life sets a person on rather than just the final outcome. It is the small losses and victories along the way that build character as opposed to one major, life-altering event. That event may be the catalyst for change and character-building, but it is not usually the ultimate end-all of the experience. Instead, the daily struggles against a person's own shortcomings to reach a larger, greater purpose is where character arises.

Key Takeaway 5

Having a vocation is an integral part of life and building character, but the vocation must be correctly focused and done with pure, selfless dedication.

Analysis

For many who believe in constructing a life around good character, a vocation is an intrinsic part of that maturation. Without a true calling or vocation, life may not have the meaning necessary to determine what character means for that particular person. Vocation is serving not just a need that a person determines is best served by them, but rather by a specific need determined by the community that requires the talents that a certain person possesses.

An important component of vocation is dedication not solely to the community but to the work itself. Dedication to the people a person serves could mean distracting thoughts about whether or not the people he serves accept or appreciate his efforts. If that person instead focuses on the work rather than the community the work is for, he will inevitably serve the community in his best capacity by not allowing the opinions of the community to have impact on what needs to be done.

The Road to Character | A Review

Another key component of a vocation is a pure dedication to the cause rather than someone who has an idealistic perspective or someone who is out to do something noteworthy for themselves. On the way to building character, people must adhere to a selflessness and not succumb to a sense of self-righteousness for what they are doing. People can be caught up in their own heroism or can be corrupted by their own self-righteousness. Without self-restraint, good intentions can turn into an instrument that serves the good-doer's vanity rather than the community. People in groups can be overly smug, dogmatic, single-minded, vain, and otherwise compelled to make morally tainted choices in the name of power attained en route to bettering the community.

Key Takeaway 6

A common element in building character is to practice self-discipline, self-restraint, and self-control.

Analysis

One of the most common threads throughout the book was the selected individuals' ways of practicing self-discipline, self-restraint, and self-control, all of which played out in a variety of ways from person to person. Characters, like Dorothy Day, believe that man in his pure form is corrupt and can only be saved by suppressing natural urges. Others, like George Marshall, found that self-discipline was the best way to overcome adversity and to triumph not only in life itself but in mental and emotional aptitude in response to life. A. Phillip Randolph and his mentee, Bayard Rustin, practiced nonviolence in their work in the civil rights movement, which took its own breed of self-discipline in a time of corruption, fury, and utter disregard for humanity. George Eliot, who publicly renounced her faith, eventually found that even she should temper her impulses for the good of her family and the social fabric of her community. All of these individuals found intrinsic ways to develop character through strengthening acts of self-restraint, self-discipline, and self-control.

Along with self-discipline comes the virtue of moderation, a virtue that is often misunderstood as merely finding the middle ground between two opposing sides. Instead, a person who is moderate understands that conflict is inevitable. To live a life driven by character, a moderate person finds a way to balance both sides rather than simply find a midpoint. At times, a situation will need free rein and, at other times, a modicum of control. However, this delicate balance is struck only when a moderate understands completely that no single answer exists, but rather a series of options for ways to balance the two sides.

This moderation extends not only to outward situations but to the inner self as well. Whether weighing personal opinion toward policy versus the policy itself, or community versus individualism, a moderate works through that same delicate balance within to achieve a clearer perception and produce more thoughtful reactions. The moderate person also understands that those perceptions and reactions will change based on the situation, but always strives for a mental balance.

Key Takeaway 7

Self-mastery is an illusion. People need to find external outlets for their emotions and receive help along the way from family, friends, role models, strangers, and institutions to build true character.

Analysis

While many people feel that they are in complete control over their present circumstances and destinies, self-mastery is but an illusion that presents itself at many turns. Suffering is one of the clearest examples of self-mastery in denial. In suffering, a person cannot tell himself to stop feeling pain or to halt any particular emotion as much as that person might mentally struggle to contain it. He cannot completely separate himself from that thought or emotion internally though he may excel in hiding its outward effects. The healing process from any source of suffering is also more often than not out of an individual's control, as thoughts and emotions change with time, but not necessarily in the way or at the rate that the individual desires.

However, instead of focusing on mastering the self, that person should focus on how to master his response to a particular situation or stimulus. This effort confronts the self at a deeper level by surrendering control of thought and emotion instead centering efforts on what that person can control, which is a thought-out response. Here is another point where character can be built. Instead of lashing out or reacting without any prior thought, a carefully concocted response can bring about solutions to a problem and tranquility for both the individual and anyone else involved. Even better, that person can derive a way to redeem a negative situation into a positive response that can serve others and alleviate pain from similar experiences by other people. In giving up attempts to master the self in the moment, a person can develop the character necessary to offer a fraternal way to connect with the community and, simplistically, turn something bad into something good.

As another integral way to overcome the inability to master the self, people can rely on others, such as friends, family members, even strangers and institutions. All of these may offer not only solace but inspiration to do something more with the thoughts and emotions burning inside. This can, again, be outward in terms of helping others. It can also mean simply sharing thoughts with another person and allowing that person to offer consolation, counsel, and support to help in a time of need, a time that may inevitably build character by overcoming it.

Key Takeaway 8

Guidance and inspiration from exemplars and institutions enables people to conquer self-limitations and work on building character.

Analysis

As George Marshall displayed utmost reverence and veneration of his mentors and the leaders who came before him, so too must those in search of developing character venerate the exemplars in their own lives. Without mentors, leaders, and exemplars, people do not have standards to abide by or compare themselves to, so true greatness is measured only with much difficulty and subjectivity. Imitating the actions of exemplars is a necessary focus to bring about positive change in a person's life.

In addition to exemplary people, institutions can be models for building character. In modern times this may be less so, as many people doubt the integrity of many different institutions, from corporations and governments to charities and religion. Institutional anxiety lurks about, particularly in younger generations, and distrust mounts with each passing scandal. However, for a long time institutions were revered for the foundations they provided and examples that came out of those institutions, whom people could revere for their good character.

Nowadays, institutions are barred from consciousness in lieu of individualism and nonconformance. In this way, it is not the institutions that are revered, but the good people who surface from them and earn widespread respect. As an example, people tend to look to startups for business savvy and creative inspiration rather than established corporations that people might believe are out only for financial gains.

The next step in building character, once a person has properly drawn from the inspiration of the great men and women who came before him, is to become a model citizen and exemplar to others. To personify a heralded figure and transcend that imitation into building an inspirational character of his own, a person can embody any definition of character, classical or modern. While leaving behind a legacy should not be a person's motivation for goodness, focusing solely on the cause or task at hand with no shroud of self-righteousness or desire for fame and fortune, a person can become the very model of goodness that his own exemplars were to him.

Key Takeaway 9

Without love, whether it be romantic, familial, religious, or humanitarian, people cannot develop the traits or have the experiences needed to build character.

Analysis

Love performs a number of roles on the journey to building character. Love is a humbling force that demonstrates the necessity of others to truly have an effect on refining a person's personality. Love also reminds people that they are not truly in control of themselves or their destinies, as love can affect every fiber of a person's being, transforming their hopes, dreams, wants, and needs in relation to the object of that love and affection.

In this way, love means surrendering to another person, exposing vulnerabilities and giving up on attempts to master the self. Love removes a person's focus from himself and translates that focus into something tangible felt for another person, forcing people away, at least in part, from self-love. Love means submission to another without counting costs.

Love impels people to act rather than remain complacent. Sometimes this action is negative and drives people to make poor decisions. Other times, love motivates people to do better, live better, and contribute more of themselves to others and the community. A person's love for a child may compel them to start a charity drive for children in need. A person's love for a family member battling an illness may create a foundation to serve other people and their families who are also battling the same disease. Love moves and inspires people to do something better with their lives and to become a better version of themselves, all of which leads people down the path to good character.

Key Takeaway 10

Overcoming pride is another essential aspect of the psychological overhaul needed to develop character.

Analysis

Pride has both positive and negative connotations, but in the context of *The Road to Character*, pride is seen as an obstacle to developing character. In some circles, pride is seen as a benefit, wherein a prideful person feels good about himself, his accomplishments, and his associations. Taking pride in something can be seen as something admirable, something that means a person dedicates his entire mental, emotional, and physical being to some task or cause, and that pride often shows in the success of that effort.

However, pride can easily step over the invisible line between character benefit and character flaw. In a negative connotation, pride is often associated with someone who is arrogant and egotistical, who insufferably boasts and flaunts his talents and successes. In another negative version of pride not commonly associated with the term, people with low self-esteem demonstrate the exact opposite of conventional pride but are still afflicted by the same root cause. In both cases, accomplishments and happiness are inextricably linked, but this is not how character is built.

In many cases, pride is seen as a vice and barrier to development of self-restraint. Pride blinds people to their weaknesses and closes their minds to outside criticisms or any inkling that they could be wrong or less wonderful than they deem themselves. As people need to depend on love of and experience with others, pride is a divisive tool that separates the prideful from their beloved. Pride makes people cruel and insensitive to others' plights and ignores the fact that no one can write their own story without the people and institutions behind them that build true greatness and a real sense of character. If people can overcome pride through self-restraint, modesty, moderation, and introspection, developing good character is much closer within grasp.

Style Analysis

David Brooks uses several different types of resources to form his biographical depictions of the individuals in his book. They all share one common thread, finding a road to character. The author begins with a general examination of the definition of character, moral ecology, and what character-building looks like before launching into his first story. Then he introduces concepts that he will reference throughout the book, such as Adam 1 versus Adam 2.

From there he develops his character portraits, limiting each chapter to focus on one or at most a few individuals. If he tells more than one character story, they usually play a supporting role to the overarching narrative of the chapter that actually does focus on one key person. The author describes these chapters as moral essays that each communicate certain standards by which character can and should be built. Within each chapter are several sections, each short and simple with just a word or two, identifying a particular character trait or theme that the chapter's main character will emulate in the stories and personality analyses that followed.

The Road to Character | A Review

To tell these stories, the author draws from biographical history that he gleans from the individuals' biographies or news stories. He also uses sentiments from these biographies as personality descriptions rather than just hard facts. Many of these individuals were writers in some capacity, whether it be in diary or letter form, that the author pulls from as well. The author includes snapshots of the individuals' lives or personalities as told through the eyes of people close to them, such as family members, friends, and coworkers, that are also referenced from diaries or letters. He also uses sentiments of character and character traits written by other authors and luminaries throughout the book.

The author chose a cast of individuals who could not have been more different in terms of their backgrounds, struggles, and ultimate transformations. He weaves their stories together by drawing parallels to a journey to develop character, namely that all characters had to descend to the valleys of struggle, develop humility and self-restraint, dedicate themselves to a cause bigger than themselves, and ascend to the heights of exemplary character. The author wraps these themes up in a final chapter.

Perspective

David Brooks is a journalist, media personality, and teacher who draws upon his skills as a reporter to research and share the stories of these individuals. In the beginning of the book, he mentions his own path to improve his moral vocabulary as he took the journey in researching and writing these narratives. Through his self-discovery, he was able to paint a picture of current society's moral ecology and compare it to those of the past societies he wrote about.

Made in the USA
Lexington, KY
10 September 2016